Who Am I to Judge?

Loveland, Colorado

Group's R.E.A.L. Guarantee to you:
This Group resource incorporates our R.E.A.L. approach to ministry—one that encourages long-term retention and life transformation. It's ministry that's:

Relational
Because learner-to-learner interaction enhances learning and builds Christian friendships.

Experiential
Because what learners experience through discussion and action sticks with them up to 9 times longer than what they simply hear or read.

Applicable
Because the aim of Christian education is to equip learners to be both hearers and doers of God's Word.

Learner-based
Because learners understand and retain more when the learning process takes into consideration how they learn best.

Note:
The price of this text includes the right for you to make as many copies of the studies as you need for your immediate church group. If another church or organization wants copies of these studies, it must purchase *Christian Character Development Series: Who Am I to Judge?* for its own use.

Christian Character Development Series: Who Am I to Judge?

Copyright © 2000 and 2002 Group Publishing, Inc.

2002 edition

All rights reserved. No part of this book may be reproduced in any manner whatsoever without prior written permission from the publisher, except where noted in the text and in the case of brief quotations embodied in critical articles and reviews. For information, write Permissions, Group Publishing, Inc., Dept. PD, P.O. Box 481, Loveland, CO 80539.

Visit our Web site: www.grouppublishing.com

Credits
Contributing Authors: Cris Alsum, Tim Baker, Erin McKay, Siv M. Ricketts, and Jane Vogel
Book Acquisitions Editor: Julie Meiklejohn
Editor: Debbie Gowensmith
Creative Development Editor: Paul Woods
Chief Creative Officer: Joani Schultz
Copy Editor: Betty Taylor
Art Director: Randy Kady
Cover Art Director: Jeff A. Storm
Computer Graphic Artist: Pat Miller
Cover Design: Alan Furst, Inc. Art and Design
Illustrator: Amy Bryant
Production Manager: Peggy Naylor

Unless otherwise noted, Scripture taken from the HOLY BIBLE, NEW INTERNATIONAL VERSION®. Copyright © 1973, 1978, 1984 by International Bible Society. Used by permission of Zondervan Publishing House. All rights reserved.

ISBN 0-7644-2430-0
10 9 8 7 6 5 4 3 2 1   11 10 09 08 07 06 05 04 03 02

Printed in Canada.

Contents

Introduction 4

How to Use This Book 4

Other Topics 6

The Studies

   1. One True Thing 7
      Because Jesus is the truth and the source of absolute truth, we can determine what's morally right and wrong.

   2. Peer Pressure 16
      God will help us do what is right in the face of peer pressure.

   3. Which Way Do I Go? 22
      God will guide us in making good decisions.

   4. The Reality of Sex 28
      Sex is a gift from God to be enjoyed in a marriage relationship.

   5. Breaking Inner Conflict 35
      God wants us to turn away from drugs and alcohol and toward him.

   6. Holy Filtering 42
      God wants us to be aware of the things that influence our minds and hearts.

   7. He's Got the Whole World in His Hands 49
      We can trust God to give us rest during our times of stress.

   8. First Things First 57
      God wants to be first in our lives.

Introduction

Our teenagers may be talking the talk, but are they walking the walk? Often an enormous gap exists between the Christian values many teenagers claim to have and their actions. Take a moment to ponder these sobering statistics:

- Six out of ten Christian teens say there is no such thing as absolute truth.
- One out of four deny the notion that acting in disobedience to God's laws brings about negative consequences.
- One-half believe the main purpose of life is enjoyment and personal fulfillment.
- Almost half contend that sometimes lying is necessary.

What's wrong with this picture?

Today's teenagers face more choices than any teenagers before them have. They are asked to interpret, evaluate, and make moral decisions within a culture that ignores morality and changes rapidly. The choices your teenagers make today have eternal consequences. Can their faith keep up?

How can we help? We can begin by taking them on a journey—a journey toward stronger, more Christlike character. As teenagers learn to interpret and evaluate their decisions in light of their relationships with God, they will discover the importance of living out their faith in everything they do.

How to Use This Book

Who Am I to Judge? contains eight studies, each designed to address a different moral issue teenagers face in their daily lives.

- The study about **moral absolutes** will not only help students see that God determines right and wrong for everybody, but also will lead students in discerning what those truths are.
- The study about **peer pressure** will lead students to experience the benefits of fighting negative peer pressure and engaging in positive peer pressure.

- In the study about **making good decisions,** students will seek God's help in making decisions in their lives and will learn about tools for doing so.

- The study about the **sex** will encourage students to view sex as a gift from God that forms a union between two people; therefore they'll learn that treating sex casually creates problems only God can address through forgiveness.

- In the study about **drugs and alcohol,** students will consider how drugs and alcohol feed the sinful nature and how the freedom God offers helps us live by the Spirit.

- The study about **media and music** will provide students with tools for filtering the messages they receive through different media.

- The study about **handling stress** will show students that focusing on God rather than on themselves will help them rest in God's peace.

- The study about **idolatry** will encourage students to look at their own lives for "hidden" idols that steer their focus away from God.

The Christian Character Development Series encourages students to examine their own character in a very individual, personal way. Each study in this series guides students to examine the topic individually, in pairs, and in larger groups.

Each study connects the topic and the Scriptures to God-centered character development—the idea that God gives us a model of quality character in his Word, as well as a desire to know him and to become more like him.

Before each study, photocopy the entire study for each person. Each person in your group will have his or her own set of handouts to use extensively throughout each study for journaling and other writing and drawing activities. Each study begins with a section called "Read About It" and then follows with a section called "Write About It." These sections provide teenagers with "food for thought" about the topic and provide the opportunity to respond to those thoughts, right on their papers. You may choose to have your students complete these sections before your group meets, or you may decide to have students complete these sections at the beginning of your meeting time.

Other sections of the study are designed so students can work through them with a minimum of direction from you. Any direction you may need to give your students is included in the "Leader Instructions" boxes. You're encouraged to participate and learn right along with the students—your insights will enhance students' learning.

Each study provides a combination of introspective, active, and interactive learning. Teenagers learn best by experiencing the topic they're learning about and then sharing their thoughts and reactions with others.

The Christian Character Development Series will help you guide your teenagers through the perils and pitfalls of growing up in today's culture. Use the studies in this book to work with your youth to understand what it means to have high standards of character and to learn why character is important to God.

Other Topics

Who Am I With Others?
Knowing God
Conflict
Forgiveness
Friendships
Parents and Other Authorities
Dating
Loneliness
Love

Who Am I When Nobody's Looking?
Honesty
Wisdom
Integrity
Humility
Trust
Generosity
Compassion
Faithfulness

Who Am I Inside?
Hope
Fear
Guilt
Pride
Joy
Grief
Anger
Peace

Who Am I to God?
Salvation
The Bible
The Trinity
Prayer
Service
Faith
Sharing Faith
Worship

Who Am I...Really?
Righteousness
Popularity
Success
Self-Esteem
The Family of God
Spiritual Gifts
Role Models and Heroes
The Future

One True Thing

✠ **Because Jesus is the truth and the source of absolute truth, we can determine what's morally right and wrong.**

Supplies: You'll need Bibles, pens or pencils, and concordances.

Preparation: Set out the supplies on a table to use during the study.

Leader Instructions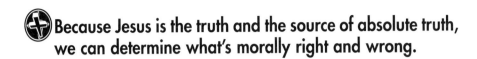

Begin by having students each read the "Read About It" section and respond in the "Write About It" section.

Read About It

In the book *Right From Wrong,* Josh McDowell and Bob Hostetler outline two ways of looking at truth:

"Model #1: Truth is defined by God for everyone; it is objective and absolute.

"Model #2: Truth is defined by the individual; it is subjective and situational.

According to Model #1, God is in authority over everyone, and God defines what is right and wrong. According to Model #2, each person has authority over his or her own life and can define what is right and wrong at any time.

Write About It

• Which model of truth do you most agree with? Why?

_____
_____
_____
_____
_____

- Which model do you think is most accepted in society today? How do you see that model operating in the way people think or act?

- How might morality be affected by society's view of truth? What examples support your opinion? What examples might someone use to argue against your opinion?

Experience It

Leader Instructions

Have students form groups of four to work through the "Moral Absolutes" pages (pp. 9-11). Bring the groups together after they've completed each section to report their responses and for clarification of any confusion about the process.

Tell Me More...

"We cannot separate the principle of truth from the Person who embodies it: Jesus Christ. A relationship with Jesus Christ is the integrating factor that makes it possible not only to understand truth, but to apply it to your life and relationships, to issues of morality and ethics and politics and all sorts of things."

—Josh McDowell and Bob Hostetler, *Right From Wrong*

Moral Absolutes

Depends on Who You Ask

Assign one of the statements below to each member in your group.

- I live before Christ, and everyone knows it's OK to have more than one wife; in fact, the women would be destitute otherwise, so the men are doing the women a favor.
- It's the early 1800s, and everyone where I live knows that owning slaves is simply necessary for business.
- In my culture, everyone knows that people are born into different classes and that higher classes just shouldn't mix with lower classes.
- Today everyone knows that you can't restrict sex and violence on TV, in the movies, or on the Internet without gutting our free-speech rights.

Each person in your group should take thirty seconds to argue the point he or she was assigned as if the person believes it. Afterward, each person should take an additional thirty seconds to argue against the point.

In your group, discuss these questions and write your answers in the space provided:

- Is the view that "everyone's doing it" a valid measure of right or wrong?

- Does truth change depending on the individual, time period, culture, and society? Explain.

- Do you think one of the opinions you pretended to support is really the only right opinion? How can you know?

Truth

In your group, read the following passages and jot down a summary of what each passage teaches about God's moral character and about truth. Then discuss the questions, and write your answers in the space provided.

- Deuteronomy 32:4

- John 14:6-7

- James 1:17

- If God is just, can do no wrong, is the truth, and doesn't change, how does God compare to "everybody's doing it" as a measure of right or wrong?

In the squares below, draw a comparison between God as a measure of right and wrong and society as a measure of right and wrong.

God

Society

- How can you use this information to help you determine whether there is one right opinion about the situations above? Explain.

Moral Principles

With your group members, fill in the chart below with some examples of God's character and the resulting moral principles. The first one has been completed as an example.

Passage	God's Character	Moral Principle
John 14:6-7	God is truth.	Moral behavior must be truthful.
Deuteronomy 7:9; 2 Timothy 2:13	God is	Moral behavior must be
1 John 3:3	God is	Moral behavior must be
1 John 4:8	God is	Moral behavior must be

- How does this process influence your understanding of the relationship between God's character and our moral choices?

- How can this process help you determine whether there is one right opinion about the situations above—or any situation? Explain.

Moral Choices

In your group, use the process you learned in the "Moral Principles" section to try to figure out whether the following statements are right or wrong, no matter what. Use this chart to help you, and look in a concordance if you need further help.

Statement	Bible Verses	God's Character	Moral Principle	Resulting Decision
I live before Christ, and everyone knows it's OK to have more than one wife; in fact, the women would be destitute otherwise, so the men are doing the women a favor.				
It's the early 1800s, and everyone where I live knows that owning slaves is simply necessary for business.				
In my culture, everyone knows that people are born into different classes and that higher classes just shouldn't mix with lower classes.				
Today everyone knows that you can't restrict sex and violence on TV, in the movies, or on the Internet without gutting our free-speech rights.				

After you've filled out the chart, discuss these questions and write your answers in the space provided.

- What problems arise when everyone operates from his or her own version of truth?

- What difference would it make if everyone agreed on a standard—a way to know what's absolutely morally right and wrong?

- What's the difference between going through this process and going through a list of rules—do's and don'ts?

- What are your ideas for refining this process? How could you make this process work for you in your own life?

Apply It

In your small group, talk about four specific moral choices that you or people you know struggle with. Being as detailed as possible, write each dilemma on the "Real-Life Choices" page (p. 13) under "the problem." Write your problems

- as a question—for example, "Is it wrong to smoke if you're below the legal age for buying cigarettes?"
- as a case study—for example, "Tom was taking a geometry test when he noticed Alice looking at his paper..."
- as a request for advice—for example, "What should I do if..."

When you've finished, give your books to another group. When you've received up to four books from another group, discuss the dilemmas the group wrote about. In each book, complete the "moral principles" and "some responses" sections of the page.

Tell Me More...

Understanding the principle behind a decision can help you avoid legalism and judgmentalism. For example, in Mark 7:1-8, the Pharisees got hung up on a man-made rule instead of the principle behind God's true commands.

Don't mistake every specific choice for a moral absolute. For example, suppose you determine that a good way to maintain your sexual purity is to go on group dates rather than to date only as a couple. Is this a valid decision that supports the moral absolute of purity? Yes. Is group dating a moral absolute for all people in all times and places? Obviously not.

Tell Me More...

You may not feel you know God's character well enough to discern principles that will guide your choices. Don't be discouraged! Two simple questions can help you:

- What is the loving thing to do? (Remember, God is love and Jesus told us that the two greatest commandments flow from that characteristic: Love God, and love other people.)
- What would Jesus do?

Real-Life Choices

The Problem

Describe a real-life moral choice that you or people you know face.

A different group will complete the rest of this page.

The Moral Principles

Based on what you know about God's *character* (remember the difference between rules and principles), what moral principles do you think apply in this situation?

Some Responses

What possible response(s) to the problem would the moral principles lead to?

Leader Instructions

Have groups present the problems and responses to the other groups. After each, ask:

- *How does this response reflect the character of God?*
- *What other responses would you suggest?*
- *What would the different responses say about your character?*

After the presentations, close with prayer, asking God to guide everyone toward the good choices God's character can help him or her make.

Live It

Monday: Read James 1:16-27.

Tuesday: Read James 1:16-27. What does it mean that God "chose to give us birth through the word of truth"? (See Ephesians 1:13 and Colossians 1:5-6.)

Extension Idea

You may wish to have groups role play the problems and possible responses.

Wednesday: Read James 1:16-27. Have you experienced the birth that verse 18 mentions? If so, how does it influence your character—who you really are? If you're not sure you've experienced it, who could you talk to about it? Call that person this week.

Thursday: Read James 1:16-27. Underline all the words that relate to truth or deception. What do you learn from this passage about truth?

Friday: Read James 1:16-27. What do you learn about God's character? List all the words that describe God.

Saturday: Read James 1:16-27. What do you learn about moral character?

Sunday: Read James 1:16-27. List the instructions God gives you in this passage. Next to each, rate yourself with a plus or a minus. In which ones do you need to ask God to help you change?

Peer Pressure

 God will help us do what is right in the face of peer pressure.

Supplies: You'll need Bibles, pens or pencils, a small paper bag, concordances, and six index cards—three with the word "positive" written on each of them and three with the word "negative" written on each of them.

Preparation: Place the index cards in the paper bag, then set out the supplies on a table to use during the study.

Leader Instructions

Begin by having students each read the "Read About It" section and respond in the "Write About It" section.

Read About It

Calee had never done anything like this before. She tried to do the right things. She went to church, youth group, and special church events. She tried to be nice to her friends and family. She read her Bible a few times a week.

But tonight she felt tired of doing the right thing. She wanted to do what everyone else was doing. So she lied to her parents, telling them she was going to spend the night at Rachel's house. Then she and Rachel went to a big party at the abandoned warehouse on the edge of town.

At first, Calee felt a rush of excitement as she held a drink in her hand and looked around at all the people having fun. She felt like part of the crowd.

But then the feeling faded as she thought about her parents. They had trusted her, and she wasn't anywhere near Rachel's house. What if she got caught? What if she didn't get caught but the horrible, guilty feeling in the pit of her stomach didn't go away? Was it worth it?

Write About It

- How do you respond when you're faced with pressure to do something you know is wrong?

_____

_____

- Define "peer pressure."

- What would you say to Calee if you were trying to influence her with negative peer pressure? with positive peer pressure?

- Read 1 Corinthians 15:33. In what ways does Calee's situation portray what Paul warns about here? What does the kind of company we keep have to do with peer pressure?

Experience It

Leader Instructions

Have students form up to six groups, and point out the supply table you've prepared before the study.

As students begin the "Facing the Pressure" pages, have each group choose a different scenario to act out. Have a representative from each group draw an index card from the bag.

In your group, follow the instructions on the "Facing the Pressure" pages (pp. 18-19).

Tell Me More...

"No matter what age we are, we can expect to face negative peer pressure from the day we are born to the day we die. Each of us will experience it in different ways and degrees, depending on our own life experience, peer group, and self-image."

—Walt Mueller, *Understanding Today's Youth Culture*

Facing the Pressure

Read the scenarios below; your leader will help you determine which scenario you'll work on. After you've chosen your scenario and an index card, read the Scriptures below, discuss the questions, and write your answers in the space provided.

Psalm 1:1-2

- What does this psalm teach you about negative peer pressure?

    that you're not blessed if you're walking un godly

- What kinds of actions and words communicate negative peer pressure?

Hebrews 10:24-25

- What does this Scripture teach you about positive peer pressure?

    that we should encourage each other & love each other

- What kinds of actions and words communicate positive peer pressure?

    encourage

Matthew 4:1-11

the devil tempted Jesus with the things

- How was the pressure Jesus faced similar to the pressure teenagers face?

    James 4:7-8   that mattered — (Devil isn't going to tempt you to eat celery.)

- How did Jesus respond to that pressure?

    Combated devil with scripture

- From Jesus' response, what can you apply to situations in which you face pressure?

Prepare to act out your group's scenario to portray either positive or negative peer pressure, depending on the card you drew. Just as Jesus used God's Word to determine his actions, find Scriptures that would help someone in the situation your group portrays know what to do. For example, if your scenario involves pressure to gossip about classmates, you could use James 3:1-12 to

If were holding on to both lies the devil has his foot in your spiritual door. And you will always have trouble with peer pressure & temptation. — Resist & he will flee

18 ◆ Study 2

determine the right thing to do. You may want to use a concordance to help you. Below the scenario, write the Scriptures you find. Everyone in your group should participate in the presentation, and at least one character in your presentation should use Scripture.

Scenarios

- You and your friend have been invited to the biggest party of the year. You know people will be drinking there. What would you do?

- Your neighbor recently bought some spray paint and plans to use it to "decorate" your school. He has invited you to join him in his plans. What would you do?

- You've been seeing your boyfriend for more than six months, and he's ready to take your physical relationship further. What would you do?

- A friend of yours has been acting quite depressed lately. After asking you to promise not to tell anyone, she commented that she had no hope and wished she were dead. What would you do?

- You're excelling at basketball and hope to make the first string next season. Your coach and teammates strongly suggest that you attend a basketball camp this summer. It will be held at the same time as the youth group mission trip you've told your parents you would attend. What would you do?

- The hottest movie of the year was just released. It's rated R. Several of your friends are going to see it, and they want you to go too. They've offered to tell your parents that you're going to a different movie. What would you do?

[handwritten: Garbage in Garbage out]

[handwritten: video - uplifting?]

Leader Instructions

After groups have finished preparing, have each take a turn presenting its scenario. Ask students to write below the scenario on the "Facing the Pressure" pages the Scripture mentioned in each presentation.

After the presentations, process the activity using questions like these:

- What tools did you learn to use for facing peer pressure? for communicating positive peer pressure?
- How can God help you in these situations?
- What other Scriptures or decisions could have worked in these scenarios?

Then have students form pairs before beginning the "Apply It" activity.

Extension Idea

Have students prepare a skit containing their scenarios to share with other youth groups or the congregation. Your group could use the skit for teaching, discipleship training, or outreach.

Apply It

With your partner, discuss areas in which you face negative peer pressure. In the space below, draw what you think might happen if you don't get God's help in standing up to that pressure.

Now choose Scriptures that will help you stand up to that pressure. See the Scriptures you wrote below each scenario on the "Facing the Pressure" page, or use a concordance to find your own. Use the space below to write the words of the Scripture you've chosen and why you chose that Scripture.

_____

_____

Next trade books with your partner, and write a short prayer for your partner. Ask God to guide your partner as he or she faces peer pressure. After writing the prayer, write one way you'll try to positively pressure your partner to face the pressure.

_____

_____

Live It

Talk to a couple of adults, who you respect, about the pressure they faced as teenagers. Were they happy with their responses? How can their responses to the pressure guide your responses?

Pressure faced	Person's response	Person's evaluation of the response	What you can learn

Pray

What are the things that tempt you
Do you feel pressure?

Which Way Do I Go?

 God will guide us in making good decisions.

Supplies: You'll need Bibles, pens or pencils, newsprint, several different colors of yarn, scissors, tape, and colored markers.

Preparation: Set out the supplies on a table to use during the study.

Leader Instructions

Begin by having students each read the "Read About It" section and respond in the "Write About It" section.

Read About It

Is it true or not?

Do you get to choose, or do other forces choose for you?

When you're in school, you may feel like you have very little control. Teachers pour on the homework. Classes and practices take up most of your day. You have chores at home and possibly a part-time job. Very little of your time is your own.

What about catastrophes like cancer diagnoses, car wrecks, or cranky teachers? And aren't some people just luckier? They get the better families, better teachers, better breaks, better education.

You, and only you, choose whether to call on God's power to move through life. It really is true. You make the moves that determine the joy or misery in your life. You choose to be spoiled or sensitive. You choose to care or to criticize. You choose to make the most of things or to waste your moments. Choose to stand for Christ.

Write About It

• What's your reaction to this quote? Does it ring true of your life? Explain.

- What criteria do you use when making decisions? Do you have general guidelines for all decisions, or do your guidelines change depending on the decision? Give examples.

_____
_____
_____

- What could help you make better decisions?

_____
_____
_____

Experience It

Leader Instructions

Have students form small groups, and point out the supply table you've prepared before the study.

In your group, follow the instructions on the "Decisions, Decisions" pages (pp. 24-25). Use the supplies on the supply table as needed.

Decisions, Decisions
Section 1

Discuss the following questions, and write the answers in the space provided.

- You make decisions all day long, every day. In one minute, brainstorm a list of decisions that the typical teenager might face in a day.

- Individually, follow these instructions:

  Put a line through any decisions you consider easy.

  Put a wavy line under decisions you consider important.

  Circle decisions you consider difficult.

  Draw a box around decisions that require moral consideration.

- Share your marks with your group. How did you decide how to mark each decision?

- Read Ephesians 5:15-17. According to this passage, how should we make decisions?

- How do you know if a decision is wise? foolish?

- How do you know what the Lord's will is?

Section 2

This time line represents your life. Think of five important decisions you've made. The line itself represents "neutral," the space above the line represents "good," and the space below the line represents "bad." Make five dots to represent your key decisions. Then connect the dots to make a decision graph.

When group members have finished, discuss these questions:

- Have you generally made good or bad decisions? Why?

- What influence do friends have on your decisions?

- Can having good friends help you make better decisions?

- Read Psalm 1:1-3. What does this passage tell us about

...the role of our friends in decision-making? _____

...the role of God's Word in decision-making? _____

...the effect of having good friends and following God's Word? _____

Section 3

Read Philippians 4:8-9. Using the criteria in these verses, how would you decide

...what movie to see? _____

...what to do on a date? _____

...what to do in your free time? _____

...what to do after high school? _____

...who to marry? _____

Section 4

Write three decisions you currently face or will face in the near future, each on its own line. Then write how you can pray about each decision on the same line.

- Read John 14:26 and Ephesians 3:14-21. How can God use prayer to help you make good decisions?

Spend a few minutes praying together for your decisions. Pass your book to the right. In the book you now hold, write a sentence prayer for the person's first decision. For example, if he or she has to decide where to go to college, you might pray that God would provide the highest amount of financial aid. Keep passing books and praying until you've written a one-sentence prayer for each of the three decisions. When you receive back your book, prayerfully read through the prayers.

Apply It

Stay in your group. Discuss these questions, and write your answers in the space provided.

- When making a decision, how do you know whether what you think you should do is God's will or not?

  _____

  _____

- How can God use the following to help you make good decisions:

Friends? _____

_____

The Bible? _____

_____

Prayer? _____

_____

Circumstances? _____

_____

- Share with your group one way God has used one of these methods to guide you in a decision, or share how God might use one or more of these methods to guide you in a current decision.

Read Colossians 2:6-7. Paul uses four metaphors to describe what it looks like to live in Christ: a plant with strong roots, a building, an athlete in training, and an overflowing cup.

- How do these metaphors relate to making good decisions?

  _____

  _____

- Which metaphor do you relate to most? Explain.

  _____

  _____

The more you live in Christ, the more God can guide you in making good decisions. On the next page, draw a picture of the metaphor you most need to develop and the area of your life in which you need to live more like Christ. Instead of drawing with lines, however, draw with words to a prayer, asking God to help you with decisions you face.

Live It

Despite arguments to the contrary, your media intake will affect your decision-making—but you can reduce its subtle influence through careful consideration. This week, do a media survey. Be aware of television, movies, music, magazines, newspapers, and advertisements, and watch and listen closely. Ask yourself these questions:

- What does this promote?
- What decisions were made?
- What criteria were used to make decisions?
- Were these decisions wise or foolish? Why?
- What might be the consequences of these decisions?
- How could the characters have made wise decisions?
- What would God think of this? Explain.

Extension Idea

If your class meets at the same time as others, arrange to visit a senior adult class, or ask some senior adults to visit your class. If possible, have each student form a pair with a senior adult. Then students can ask these pillars of experience questions such as these:

- *What decisions have been pivotal in your life?*
- *How has God guided you in making those decisions?*
- *How do you know whether guidance is from God?*
- *What advice would you give me as I look forward to major life decisions?*

Tell Me More...

Jesus said, "The thief comes only to steal and kill and destroy; I have come that they may have life, and have it to the full" (John 10:10). God wants to guide us toward good decisions, knowing that as we follow him, we will avoid many of the pitfalls of sin. Even though the wrong decisions may sometimes appear more appealing, they won't produce a blessed life.

According to Colossians 3:17, we should do all things—whatever we do—in God's name, giving him thanks. That means if we're making good decisions, all of life can also be worship. Amen!

The Reality of Sex

✚ **Sex is a gift from God to be enjoyed in a marriage relationship.**

Supplies: You'll need Bibles, pens or pencils, plastic spoons, and pipe cleaners.

Preparation: Set out the supplies on a table to use during the study.

Leader Instructions

Begin by having students each read the "Read About It" section and respond in the "Write About It" section.

Read About It

Doesn't it seem like everything that tastes good is bad for you? Consider the following:

• A cup of raw spinach has no fat; a piece of pecan pie has thirty-two grams of fat.

• Four raw radishes have five calories; one cup of vanilla soft-serve ice cream has 375 calories.

• *Six* raw onions have no fat; one cup of *light* whipping cream has seventy-four grams of fat.

• Six slices of unpeeled cucumbers have five calories; Hardee's Monster Burger has 1060 calories.

It just doesn't seem fair. You'd think we'd have a desire to eat things that are good for us. But you never hear a frustrated parent saying, "After you eat three bites of your hot-fudge sundae, you can eat a big bowl of collard greens."

Sin, including sexual sin, presents the same problem. We are called by God to be pure. He designed sex to be enjoyed and celebrated in and not before marriage. Having sex outside marriage is not only mutually damaging, it's sinful. As Christians, we're called to a standard that requires patience, strength, and endurance.

Sex is a beautiful thing. But outside of marriage, sex eventually becomes a cause for regret and pain. In the midst of the intimacy and pleasure, participants steal a piece of each other's souls, and that changes them forever.

Write About It

• In your own words, state what this quote says about sex.

_____

_____

• How can sex be good in marriage and destructive outside of marriage?

_____

_____

• Read Genesis 2:24. What does it mean to you that sex is a gift from God?

_____

_____

• What do the Bible verse and the quote say about how this gift should be handled? What happens if it's not handled that way? What happens if it is handled that way?

_____

_____

Experience It

Leader Instructions

Have students form groups of four, and point out the supply table you've prepared before the study.

In your group, follow the instructions on the "Sex and Forgiveness" pages (pp. 30-31). Use the supplies on the supply table as needed.

Tell Me More…

God isn't trying to keep us from having fun. Actually, he *loves* it when we enjoy ourselves. But God created sex for a specific purpose, and he designed sex to be a precious gift given in a marriage relationship. Hey, God wants us to have fun, but he wants us to have fun in the right context. And he doesn't want us to go around forming invisible—but very real—unions with people we aren't committed to for life. It's just not part of God's plan.

Sex and Forgiveness

Section 1

Read 1 Corinthians 6:12-20. As a group, discuss the following questions and write the answers in the space provided.

- What does this passage say about the union that forms when we have sex with someone?

- What are the consequences of creating this union before marriage?

- What happens when we break that union?

- What does the fact that we were "bought at a price" have to do with our sexual behavior?

Using the spoons and pipe cleaners, work together in pairs to create a sculpture to represent how we treat our bodies either as temples of God or as temples for the world. Your sculpture should stand alone, not lie down. When you've finished, show your sculpture to the other pair in your group. Then discuss the following questions, and write the answers in the space provided.

- What was it like to make a standing sculpture with pipe cleaners and spoons? How was that similar to the difficulty of avoiding sexual immorality?

- Take apart your sculpture. How do the pipe cleaners represent how we're different after we've had sex with someone?

Section 2

Read 2 Corinthians 5:17-19. As a group, discuss the following questions and write the answers in the space provided:

- What does this passage say about forgiveness?

- How might we get rid of our old selves?

As a group, write a story of forgiveness from God's perspective, including someone's sin, God's feelings or actions as he forgives someone, and the person's response to that forgiveness.

Now share your story with another group. When you've finished, discuss these questions in your own group and write your answers in the space provided:

- How might a person's behavior change in gratitude for God's forgiveness?

- What might it mean to someone who's sinned sexually that God's forgiveness washes us clean?

- What is your response to God for forgiving you?

Leader Instructions

After groups have finished the "Sex and Forgiveness" pages, process the experience using questions like these:

- What insights have you gained from this experience?
- How has your perspective on sex changed as a result of this study?
- What new idea have you learned about God's forgiveness as a result of this study?

Extension Idea

For the second section of the "Sex and Forgiveness" activity, groups could role play how they might counsel someone who's interested in receiving God's forgiveness. Encourage groups to include 1 John 1:8-9 in their role-plays.

Apply It

Find a partner, and together read Romans 12:1-2. Then discuss the following questions, and write your answers in the space provided.

- What are some ways you can "offer your bodies as living sacrifices" instead of offering them to sexual immorality?

_____

_____

- What practical things can you do to avoid sexual immorality—going out with groups, for example?

_____

Now trade books with your partner. Fill out the prayer form below for your partner, and then spend a few moments praying for each other. After you've prayed, return the books.

Dear God,
I'm asking you to help _____ flee sexual immorality.
Help _____ to avoid sexual immorality by…

Please transform _____ by…

Give _____ the strength to…

In Jesus' name, amen.

When you have your book back, write a commitment below that you'd like to make as a result of today's study. Your commitment can be something simple like "I commit to talking with an adult about sex" or something more complex. Date your commitment so you'll know when you made it. Then think of someone you can tell about your commitment—someone who will help hold you accountable. Write that person's name below, too, and don't forget to talk with him or her about your commitment this week.

Live It

Sex is a gift, and it's such a strong temptation to open that gift long before we're supposed to. God wants us to wait because this gift is best enjoyed in a marriage relationship.

Look at 1 Thessalonians 4:3-7. Rewrite this passage in your own words.

Think about all the people who might be affected if you were to have sex outside of marriage. Write your thoughts below.

In the space below, draw a picture of your future family. As you draw the picture, consider how the choices you make now will affect them.

Tell Me More...

"At first I had a dead set answer, NO, but I wasn't strong enough. Now I'm having sex. I don't want to...Again and again I ask God for forgiveness, but then I do it again. I feel trapped and don't know what to do."

—Gloria, quoted in *Please Don't Tell My Parents* by Dawson McAllister

Breaking Inner Conflict

 God wants us to turn away from drugs and alcohol and toward him.

Supplies: You'll need Bibles, pens or pencils, modeling clay, and licorice sticks.

Preparation: Set out the supplies on a table to use during the study.

Leader Instructions

Begin by having students each read the "Read About It" section and respond in the "Write About It" section.

Read About It

When I was in junior high, I went with my family to the beach at a local reservoir. My sisters and I went swimming, and my parents went golfing after dropping us off at the beach.

Among the other swimmers was a group of high school boys who were having a lot of rowdy fun in the water. They were yelling and splashing and throwing a football.

In the midst of their fun, one of the boys started yelling, "Help!" The other boys started laughing and went on with their fun, enjoying what they thought was a joke.

But it was no joke. The boy was drowning, and his friends were laughing.

Some of the other swimmers realized what was happening and swam out to rescue the boy. But by the time they got to him, it was too late. They pulled him out of the water, but he was dead.

My sisters and I watched in horror as they carried the boy away in an ambulance. We had watched someone drown, and no one had been able to save him because his friends were too busy having fun.

Write About It

• How is drowning similar to the results of drug and alcohol use?

- For a person using drugs or alcohol, how might other people act the way the boy's friends did?

- Read Psalm 71:1-3. What solution does God offer if someone is drowning due to drugs or alcohol? What solutions does the world offer?

Experience It

Leader Instructions

Have students form groups of four, and point out the supply table you've prepared before the study.

In your group, follow the instructions on the "Getting Clarity" pages (pp. 37-38). Use the supplies on the supply table as needed.

Tell Me More...

- The effects of a drug will vary depending on an individual's personality, mood, physical size, and so on.
- Since *all* drugs can cause harm, avoiding drugs is the safest thing to do.
- Both short-term and long-term health problems—including serious health problems and death—are related to drug use.
- Drugs—including legal drugs like alcohol and cigarettes—are expensive.
- Drug use can get you into trouble with the law, affecting your present and your future.
- The emotional and social problems related to drug use can harm your relationships.

Getting Clarity
Section 1

Read Galatians 5:16-17. As a group, discuss the following questions and write your answers in the space provided.

- Describe the conflict between the Spirit and the sinful nature.

___

- How can you tell when you're being directed by your sinful nature? by God?

___

- How might drugs and alcohol keep someone from living by the Spirit?

___

- What's the difference between living by the Spirit and living under the direction of drugs or alcohol?

___

Using the modeling clay, create two group sculptures: one that represents someone living by the Spirit and one that represents someone controlled by drugs and alcohol. When you've finished, share your sculptures with another group.

Section 2

Read Romans 7:14-25. As a group, discuss the following questions and write the answers in the space provided:

- When have you faced a struggle similar to the struggle Paul wrote about?

___

- What does it mean to be a slave to sin?

___

Breaking Inner Conflict ◆ 37

- How might drugs and alcohol make a person a slave to sin?

Read Romans 8:1-3, discuss these questions, and write your answers in the space provided.
- What does it mean to be set free because of Christ?

- Why would God want us to be free from the bondage of drugs and alcohol?

As a group, write a song about someone who was a prisoner of drugs and alcohol and was then set free. Be sure to include information about the person's life before and after freedom. You might want to write your lyrics to the tune of a recent popular song. When you've finished, perform the song for another group.

Section 3

Read Romans 13:11-14, discuss these questions, and write your answers in the space provided.
- How can we focus on gratifying God rather than our sinful nature?

- How can forgiveness help us turn away from drugs and alcohol?

Get a licorice stick from the supplies table. Eat the licorice, leaving an amount to represent how much you're struggling with a certain sin. Now pray to God for help with that sin. Then as you eat the rest of the licorice, imagine what your life would be like with freedom from that sin. Thank God for freeing you.

Leader Instructions

After groups have finished the "Getting Clarity" pages, process the experience using questions like these:

- *What insights have you gained from this experience?*
- *How can you remember to turn toward God and away from negative influences?*

Apply It

Find a partner, and read Galatians 5:19-21 together. Then turn to the "Growing Fruit" page (p. 40). On the "Fruit of Sin" tree, draw and label leaves to represent the different acts of the sinful nature. Circle one leaf to indicate an act of your sinful nature for which you especially want God's forgiveness and freedom. Underneath the tree, list three actions you could take to turn away from that act.

Then read Galatians 5:22-25. On the "Growing Fruit" page (p. 40), draw and label leaves to represent the different fruits of the Spirit on the "Fruit of the Spirit" tree. Discuss with your partner which fruit of the Spirit you'd especially like God's help in cultivating, and circle that leaf. Underneath the tree, list three actions you could take to cultivate that fruit.

Trade books with your partner. On the "Growing Fruit" page, write a sentence to encourage your partner to turn away from the sinful nature and to turn toward God. When you've finished, spend a few minutes praying for your partner.

Extension Idea

For the second section of "Getting Clarity," videotape the songs that groups sing. You can use the songs to teach other groups about drug and alcohol use and redemption. Or the youth can set up a display about drugs and alcohol in the church and can include a TV to play the video as part of the display.

Tell Me More...

We all need forgiveness, but so often we don't feel any different after we've asked for it. It seems to us that nothing has changed. But when we acknowledge that we've messed up, we open ourselves to one of God's miraculous processes. We've done our part to make things right with God. We might not feel changed, but something magical has taken place: In the quietest way, we've been set free. That freedom manifests itself in our relationships, our view of ourselves, our lifestyle, and even—and most especially—our love for God.

Growing Fruit

Fruit of Sin

Fruit of the Spirit

Live It

- Look on the Internet, in magazines, or on TV to find real—not fictional—results of drug and alcohol use. What results do you find?

- What attracts people to drug and alcohol use?

- Why does God care whether we get involved with drugs or alcohol?

- How might drug or alcohol use steer people away from God?

- What difference could it make in the lives of people who use drugs or alcohol if they were to accept God's love and forgiveness?

- Below, write a statement to people who use drugs or alcohol to tell them about the love, forgiveness, and freedom God offers.

NOTE: If you use drugs or alcohol, talk with a responsible adult—your pastor or a parent, for example—to find the help that's available to set you free.

Tell Me More...

"As a fact, temptations generally increase in strength tenfold after we have entered into the interior life, rather than decrease. And no amount or sort of them must ever for a moment lead us to suppose we have not really found the true abiding place."
—Hannah Whitall Smith, *The Christian's Secret of a Happy Life,* quoted in *Disciplines for the Inner Life*

Holy Filtering

✞ **God wants us to be aware of the things that influence our minds and hearts.**

Supplies: You'll need Bibles, Bible concordances, pens or pencils, empty glasses, pitchers of water, toilet paper, coffee filters, dictionaries, and markers.

Preparation: Set out the supplies on a table to use during the study.

Leader Instructions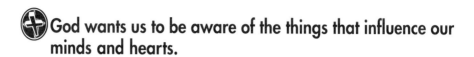

Begin by having students each read the "Read About It" section and respond in the "Write About It" section.

Read About It

Staryeyed: Media is bad when they give too much attention to the negative.

Rugman: I think [a lot of the] media is good. It influences your world view. And it helps you understand that your viewpoint isn't the only one.

Jenny932: I think it's good; it lets you know what's going on in the world nowadays and how [our] society looks at things.

RCali18: I think media is very good…It informs you on anything that will keep you glued to their station.

Jenny932: Music to me is what you make it out to be, it's not good or bad…A lot of teenagers, I think, see too much in music, they don't just enjoy it, they feel as if they need to go out and prove a point.

Pencilneck: You have to be VERY careful about media. I mean, if you don't like something, turning off the television is my immediate response. I don't want to be influenced.

Write About It

- On this scale, with ten being "a lot" and one being "not at all," rate how much you think the following media influence our culture. Use a different symbol for music, the Internet, movies, TV, and video games.

```
1   2   3   4   5   6   7   8   9   10
|___|___|___|___|___|___|___|___|___|
```

- How can music and media make our culture better? worse?

_____

_____

- How can you tell the difference between good and bad media influences?

_____

_____

- What effects do music and media have on you?

_____

_____

Experience It

Leader Instructions

Have students form groups of four, and point out the supply table you've prepared before the study.

In your group, follow the instructions on the "Shaping Influences" pages (pp. 44-45). Use the supplies on the supply table as needed.

Shaping Influences

Section 1

Read 2 Corinthians 7:1. As a group, discuss the following questions and write the answers in the space provided:

- What things might contaminate body and spirit?

- What media influences would you consider contaminants? Explain.

- How can we purify ourselves from these contaminants?

- How does this purification show reverence for God?

Using the art supplies, draw two cartoons of someone struggling with contaminating influences. The first should show someone who's given in to these influences, and the other should show someone who's resisted the influences. Include in your cartoons some influences that your group considers negative and positive. When you've finished, show your cartoons to another group.

When you've finished, discuss these questions in your group and write your answers in the space provided.

- Which cartoon panel do you relate to more? Why?

- How can we know when we've been negatively influenced?

Section 2

Read 1 Peter 1:13. As a group, discuss the following questions and write your answers in the space provided:

- Why does God want us to be careful with what we allow into our minds?

- How does "prepare your minds for action" help us know what influences are OK?

- How can we filter the media for inappropriate influences?

In your group, set two glasses so everyone can see them. Place several sheets of toilet paper over one glass and a coffee filter over the other. Slowly pour water through each filter. Watch to see how each filter performs its job. Then discuss these questions, and write your answers in the space provided:

- Which filter worked best? Why?

- What filters in life are like the toilet paper? like the coffee filter?

- What can you use to help you filter media messages as well as the coffee filter did its job?

Section 3

Read 1 Peter 1:14-16. As a group, discuss the following questions and write the answers in the space provided:

- How can we conform to Christ's image rather than to media messages?

- How does holiness help us balance media influences?

As a group, look up the word "discernment" in the dictionary. Then, using a Bible concordance, look up passages that define what discernment is. Summarize those definitions below, and write a few practical suggestions for using discernment in your life.

Scripture

Definition

Practical suggestions

Leader Instructions

After groups have finished the "Shaping Influences" pages, process the experience using questions like these:

- What are some insights you've gained from this experience?
- How can you avoid negative influences?

Extension Idea

For the third section of the "Shaping Influences" pages, have groups draw a picture of what discernment is. If the teenagers in your group like to draw, they'll dive right into this option.

Apply It

Find a partner, then turn to the "Wisdom Filter" page (p. 47). Above the filter, write some media influences you face each day—music, TV, and video games, for example. Under the filter on the left side, write some of the consequences you could face if you aren't successful at filtering these influences.

Trade books with your partner. On the right side of the filter, write three ways your partner could filter out negative influences from the media—"Pray before you log on to the Internet," for example. Then again trade books, and take time to read your partner's comments. Circle one filter idea you'd like to put into practice this week. Close by praying for God to help you both with your commitments.

Tell Me More...

Imagine that you've been feeling sick for a week and have decided to see a doctor. You finally get in to see the doctor, who glances at you, gives you a handful of pills, and sends you home.

What's wrong with this picture? The doctor never examined you but instead looked on the surface and made a snap judgment.

In order to stay spiritually healthy, we need to examine every influence with the same scrutiny with which a doctor examines a patient. We need to look closely at the things we watch and listen to; we should ask difficult questions about them. Will they bring us closer to God? Will they feed us messages that are counter to God's messages?

Being careful is not the same as being prudish or boring. It's about knowing what will hurt our relationship with God and kicking it out of our lives.

Wisdom Filter

Holy Filtering ◆ 47

Live It

- What media do you use regularly? Include specific TV shows, Internet sites, video games, and so on.

- What messages are these media giving you?

- Based on what you've learned in the study, how do these messages influence your relationship with God?

- What changes could you make in your consumption of media that would benefit your relationship with God?

He's Got the Whole World in His Hands

 We can trust God to give us rest during our times of stress.

Supplies: You'll need Bibles, pens or pencils, newsprint, several newspapers, scissors, tape, and colored markers.

Preparation: Set out the supplies on a table to use during the study.

Leader Instructions

Begin by having students each read the "Read About It" section and respond in the "Write About It" section.

Read About It

According to the American Academy of Family Physicians, about 60 percent of the problems brought to physicians in the United States are stress-related. According to *The Doctors' Guide to Instant Stress Relief*, stress can cause migraine headaches, rashes, difficulty breathing, heart and chest pain, gaseousness, and even belching. Stress can also cause depression, forgetfulness, frequent crying, and loneliness.

Most stress is the result of worrying about things we can't control. But can you think of any problem that's too big for God to handle? It's true that we need to be responsible for our lives. We need to do the best we can at everything we do. But that's where our job ends.

Write About It

• Describe stress.

_____

_____

_____

- True or False: When you feel stressed, you are primarily focused on yourself and your situation. Explain your answer.

- Have you ever experienced the kind of stress that literally makes you sick? Describe that experience.

- Read Matthew 11:28-30. Do you think Jesus wants us to be stressed? Explain.

- How could keeping our focus on God help us deal with stress?

Experience It

Leader Instructions

Have students form small groups, and point out the supply table you've prepared before the study.

In your group, follow the instructions on the "Me, Worried?" pages (pp. 51-53). Use the supplies on the supply table as needed.

Me, Worried?

Section 1

Your group will need a newspaper, a sheet of newsprint, scissors, and tape. Cut out pictures or headlines that represent things people worry about, and tape them to the newsprint to create a worry collage. As much as possible, keep related items together. For example, cutouts regarding school safety and schools' academic standings should be placed near each other since they both have to do with school. Be sure to leave some blank space near each section to write on later.

After about five minutes, use markers to write any other things people worry about. Then discuss these questions, and write your answers in the space provided.

- How much of the newspaper focused on things people worry about? What does that tell you about the news? about the world?

- Looking at your collage, how worried do you feel? Explain.

- Do you think people generally feel stressed or peaceful? Would you describe yourself as feeling stressed or peaceful? Explain.

- What might help you to feel more peaceful than stressed?

Take a deep breath, close your eyes, and count to ten. Do this three times, trying to empty your mind of everything that stresses you out.

Section 2

Read Matthew 6:25-34. As a group, discuss these questions and write the answers in the space provided.

- In one sentence, what is the main point of this passage?

- Jesus mentions several things about which people worry. How do they compare with the items on your collage?

- According to this passage, list all the reasons we shouldn't worry.

- Reread Matthew 6:31, in which Jesus phrases worries as questions. Title each section of your collage with a question or two that best sums up those worries. Take a few minutes to look at other groups' collages and questions. When you've finished, write here the two questions about which you worry most.

- Reread Matthew 6:33. What would it look like in your life to "seek first his kingdom and his righteousness"? How would doing so affect your stress level?

Take a deep breath, close your eyes, and count to ten. Do this three times, focusing your mind on God's kingdom and righteousness.

Section 3

Form a new group with three or four others who worry about questions similar to the ones you've written above. With your new group, read Philippians 4:4-7, discuss these questions, and write your answers in the space provided.

- What does it mean

...to rejoice?

...to be anxious?

- Can you rejoice and be anxious at the same time? Explain.

- What do people do to ease stress? Are those things effective? Explain.

- How can prayer help you deal with stress?

Spend a few minutes praying together for your concerns and for God to help you to deal with stress.

Section 4

Using the letters of the word "rejoice," written below, work together to write at least seven things for which your group can thank God. You can write things everyone in the group is thankful for or things God's doing in individual lives. When you've finished, your leader will direct you in a group prayer.

R

E

J

O

I

C

E

Leader Instructions

When students have completed their acrostics, lead them in a group prayer. Begin by saying "R" and pointing to a group, indicating that it should call out what its members wrote under "R." Point to each group so all can share. Then move on to the next letter, continuing until you've finished. Afterward, process the experience with questions like these:

- *Did spending time focused on God and reasons to rejoice affect your stress level? Explain.*
- *If you regularly rejoiced in God, what effect might that have on stress in your life?*
- *How can you work prayer and rejoicing into your life?*

Apply It

One reason people get stressed out is because they feel as if they have too much to do. Time management techniques can help you deal with your responsibilities *and* stay God-focused.

Extension Idea

One afternoon take a video camera and some extroverted students to the mall, and videotape shoppers answering these questions: "When do you feel most stressed?" and "How do you deal with stress?" Use the video as a fun and thought-provoking introduction to this topic.

Fill in the chart on the next page. In the first column, list a normal week's activities—attending school, sleeping, time with family, church, and so on. Also list activities that you should do or want to do but don't feel you have time to do.

In the second column, assign each activity an A, B, or C priority: A means extremely important, B means important, and C means not so important.

In the third column, estimate the time you spend on that activity each week.

In the fourth column, use the priority you've assigned each activity to decide whether you can decrease the amount of time spent.

In the fifth column, use the priority you've assigned each activity to decide whether you should (and can) add time to each activity.

In the last column, total how much time you will spend on that activity each week. Remember, there are only 168 hours per week!

Activity	Priority	Hours per week	-	+	=
	TOTAL =				

In your small group, take turns reading Matthew 11:28-30 to the person on your right, substituting his or her name for "you" and substituting references to Jesus for "I," "my," and so on. Continue until everyone has been blessed.

Live It

Think about the biggest cause of stress in your life. What steps could you take to deal with that issue? For example, if you're stressed about school, you could prioritize your time to get all your studying done. Below, brainstorm a list of actions. Then circle two or three actions you can begin to take this week.

_____

_____

Each day this week, take a few minutes to deal with your stress through prayer. You might find writing your prayers helpful.

Monday

_____

Tuesday

_____

_____

Wednesday

_____

Thursday

_____

Friday

_____

Saturday

_____

Sunday

_____

Tell Me More...

"It is not work that kills men; it is worry."
—Henry Ward Beecher, quoted in *Popular Quotations for All Uses*

Tell Me More...

Teenage stress can be a very serious problem, and some situations are best handled by a professional therapist. How do you know when you should recommend that a friend get help? The following signs and symptoms may indicate that a person is experiencing too much stress:
- A person has severe mood swings.
- A person is involved in "delinquent" disobedient behaviors.
- A person has expressed suicidal thoughts.
- A person has experienced "panic attacks."
- A person gets into many conflicts or fights.
- A person loses interest in things he or she used to do.
- A person performs compulsive behaviors such as hair pulling, excessive hand washing, face picking, nail biting, or other ritual behaviors.

(Adapted from "S.O.S!—Ministering to Stressed Out Students" by Scott Gibson, *The Comprehensive Guide to Youth Ministry Counseling*)

First Things First

 God wants to be first in our lives.

Supplies: You'll need Bibles, pens or pencils, magazines with pictures, glue, scissors, and five slips of paper per student.

Preparation: Set out the supplies on a table to use during the study.

Leader Instructions

Begin by having students each read the "Read About It" section and respond in the "Write About It" section.

Read About It

Most of us have heard that God should come first in our lives. We've heard Deuteronomy 5:7, in which God says, "You shall have no other gods before me." We know God should be "number one," yet a lot of things compete with God for our time and attention. We may become so wrapped up in these things that we begin to forget about God, to "put him on the back burner," so to speak.

When God gets nudged aside, it's by gods of our own making. These substitutes, or idols, take many forms. For example, achieving success might be the most important thing in a person's life. Material comfort is almost always highly sought after. Human beings are also frequently the objects of our affection.

In her book *Jesus in Blue Jeans,* Laurie Beth Jones observes that everyone worships at some kind of altar: "Wherever we are giving our utmost attention, our greatest gift of time and energy—there will our altar be. And for many of us, that altar is a cluttered one, piled high with big and little priorities that we shift from place to place, worshipping each one with our attention and devotion as needed."

Write About It

- What are some reasons for putting God first in our lives?

- How would you define "idolatry"?

- At what "altars" are you worshipping?

Experience It

Leader Instructions

Have teenagers form four groups, and point out the supply table you've prepared before the study.

In your group, follow the instructions on the "Idolatry" pages (pp. 59-61). Use the supplies on the supply table as needed.

Tell Me More...

The idolatry of Western man is humanism [an atheistic system of thought asserting that people need only themselves—the "worship" of humanity], materialism, and sex. Idolatry has an almost automatic connotation of superstition, magic, sorcery, and physical idols; but our modern gods are sophisticated, cultured, fashionable, and intellectual."

—Billy Graham, *World Aflame*

Idolatry

Section 1

In your group, read the following statistics from the 1998 *Statistical Abstract of the United States*, discuss the questions, and write your answers in the space provided.

- Number of larcenies in 1980: 7,137,000; in 1996: 7,895,000
- Amount of credit card spending in 1990: $467 billion; in 1997: $1,080 billion
- Amount of credit card debt in 1990: $243 billion; in 1997: $560 billion
- Number of bankruptcies in 1993: 918,700; in 1997: 1,317,000
- Average number of square feet in privately owned single-family homes in 1970: 1,500; in 1997: 2,150

- What do these statistics suggest about our pursuit of material things?

- What are some of the byproducts of affluence?

- When does affluence become a "bad" thing?

- Do you think these numbers would be different if our society put God first? Explain.

Section 2

In your group, read Exodus 32:1-14. Look through the magazines on the table to find pictures of modern-day idols, and glue the pictures to the calf below.

After about five minutes, find a partner from another group. Share your collage with your partner, discuss these questions, and write your answers in the space provided.

- What does our society seem to value highly?

- What similarities do you see between the actions of the Israelites and the actions of our society?

- Why do you think the Israelites chose to worship idols?

- What were the consequences of their idol worship?

- How might things have been different for the Israelites if they had put God first?

- Why do people in modern times sometimes put things before God?

- What results do people today face when they put things before God?

- How might our society be different if we put God first?

Return to your group, and share what you and your partner have discussed.

Section 3

In your group, read Exodus 32:19-20. Imagine that you're a modern-day Moses who wants to warn our society about idolatry. In the space below, write a letter to the editor of a local newspaper about the dangers of idolatry, why God should be number one, and how to show that God is number one.

Dear Editor,

Leader Instructions

After groups have completed their letters to the editor, ask them to share their letters with the large group. Then process the experience by asking questions like these:

- *Why does God deserve to be first in our lives?*
- *What keeps us from putting God first?*
- *How might your life be different if you put God first?*

Before moving to the next activity, pray that students will experience the value of putting God first in their lives.

Apply It

Leader Instructions

Have students think about how they spend a typical weekend. Time is something we all value, so how we choose to spend it can help identify what is most important to us. Afterward, give each student five slips of paper.

On each slip of paper, write something that is very important to you. You may write only one thing on each slip of paper. When you've finished, you should have written the five most important things in your life.

Leader Instructions

When students have finished with their slips of paper, have them sit in a large circle and face inward. Ask them to stop talking and imagine that they have been told they must give up one of the five important things they've listed. Give teenagers a moment to choose the thing they will give up, and then ask them to crumple up that slip of paper and toss it into the center of the circle. Then tell them they must give up another important thing, and continue in this manner until each student has only one slip of paper left. As students remain in the circle, have them think about the following questions on their own.

- Based on the slip of paper you're still holding, what do you value most?

_____

_____

- Does your schedule seem to support your claim about what's most important to you?

_____

_____

- What does the thing you value say about your relationship with God?

_____

_____

- Do you find it easy or difficult to put God first? Explain.

_____

_____

Using the calendar below, jot down what you could do every day of this coming week to put God first.

Sunday	Monday	Tuesday	Wednesday	Thursday	Friday	Saturday

Extension Idea

Distribute copies of the hymn "Praise God From Whom All Blessings Flow," and lead the class in singing it. Ask students what it means to praise God.

Extension Idea

Watch part of an inspirational video such as Questar's In His Presence. Encourage students to jot down their ideas as they watch the video and then compose their own hymn of praise.

Live It

Estimate the amount of time you spend doing various things on any given day. For example, you might spend two hours in some athletic activity, seven hours at school, and so on. Your time must add up to twenty-four hours. Fill in the pie chart below to illustrate how you spend your time.

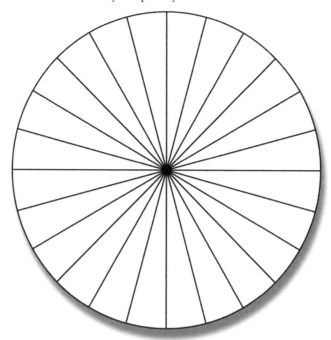

Now think about how you can put God first in each activity, and write your ideas beside the "slices" on your chart. For example, if you spend part of your day working for pay, you can put God first by working hard. If you spend part of your day practicing with a band, you can put God first by encouraging other members.

Tell Me More...

"Since [God] made us, He is in the best position to know what we need...and naturally He would want us to have these things. So He says, 'Seek ye first the Kingdom of God, and all these things will be added unto you.' It really is getting the 'cart before the horse' to aim at acquiring things, when these things may block us from the Source."

—Lake Pylant Monhollon, *The God Flow*

Tell Me More...

"Dear children, keep away from anything that might take God's place in your heart."

—1 John 5:21, *The Living Bible*